A Humorous Guide to Being a First Time Mom

Tips on pregnancy, labor and the first year of motherhood

Jessica Chamberlain

To Jenny and Davette:
Thank you for all of your support
and help on this project.

Chapter One

The Big News

The First Trimester

One day you wake up and you feel
anything but fine
You take a test and your life is changed
by a plus sign.

Sometimes it is a surprise, other times it
is by plan
Either way in nine months you'll have a
little woman or man.

In the first trimester you
may be sick and sleepy
And sometimes for no
reason, uncontrollably
weepy.

Back in college you might have paid tribute
to the
porcelain king
During pregnancy it can become a gross and
frequent thing.

Prenatal meds are important but as big as a
horse pill
Take them at night before bed to keep from
getting ill.

Drink a lot of water before each and every
check up
Because each visit begins with you peeing in
a cup.

Because of your growing baby, Tylenol is
about all you can take
Being safe rather than sorry is the best choice
you can make.

Pregnancy hormones may give you wild
dreams at night
Some are fun, wacky, intense or scary and
cause fright.

Sometimes not exercising due to pregnancy is
a treat
And watching your husband do all the chores
is really neat.

Second Trimester

In the first 20 weeks you may be full of worry
And hormones can change your mood in a
hurry.

In the second trimester you
may start to feel great
But suddenly you have gained
a ton of weight!

Your whole body will change
as you put on each pound
Your breasts grow to be
gigantic, firm and round.

When you gain weight your butt and hips
may spread
It happens to all of us so don't cry and hide in
bed.

Doctors say twenty to thirty-five pounds is
what you should gain
So eat healthy and exercise, and it will fall off
again.

Your baby will start kicking and quickly
growing in your tummy
It will let you know when something tastes
yucky or yummy.

You may place your hand on your tummy to
feel each and every kick
The mere thought of something going wrong
will be enough to make you sick.

Once your baby starts kicking it will rarely be
still
Nothing makes a baby move
like orange juice will.

If sleeping on your tummy is
your favorite way to rest
Get over it quickly because sleeping on your
left side is best.

You go in for an ultrasound to check the
heart's pace
Your own heart melts when you see your
baby's face.

As your tummy expands there will be new clothes to buy

Pregnancy is amazing and beautiful so smile don't cry.

In the middle of the night you might crave pickles and ice cream
Begging your husband to get it for you might make him want to scream.

Once you learn the gender of your baby woman or man
You will have the nursery décor, names and baby showers to plan.

The wonderful compliments, well wishes, and
gifts you receive
Will be more thoughtful and amazing than
you could ever believe.

Pamper yourself with a pedicure, a manicure
and a warm bath as a treat
But keep the water warm not hot or your baby
will overheat.

Some people think sex is
awkward and not as much
fun
It will just be a little
different because of
carrying your little one.

Sometimes water will be the only thing you
desire
It will be the one thing to help your heartburn
fire.

Around 28 weeks you will take a glucose test
If given a choice on flavors, the orange tastes
the best.

Third Trimester

As the third trimester progresses, your
anxiety may heighten
Childbirth is almost here, but there is no
reason to be frightened.

There are a few things to do in order to
prepare for the big day
Wash blankets, clothes, and get organized in
every way.

One thing you will need a lot of is jammies
Make sure to have them at home and at each
of the grammies.

Dads may think that sleeping gowns on their
boys don't look right
But they're great for changing diapers in the
middle of night.

When packing for the hospital there are a few
things you might need
But you probably won't need
all the things of which you
will read.

You might be so tired and happy that you just
don't care
But it's nice to have deodorant, shampoo and
a brush for your hair.

You will want comfy clothes for you and your
bundle of joy
A few blankets, a hat and socks for your little
girl or boy.

Your new diaper bag may come in a colored
pattern, cotton or tweed
Just make certain it has room for the million
things you will need.

Diapers, wipes, clothes and "pacis" will fill
your diaper bag
Plus bibs, bottles, toys, medicine
and a burp rag.

Orajel and teething tablets in
your diaper bag will be a must keep
When your child starts teething neither of you
will get much sleep.

Always have extra clothes for your baby and
for you
It isn't pleasant smelling like spit up or baby
poo.

Foods to avoid in pregnancy include sushi, alcohol and brie cheese
After labor you may want to say, "get me a big margarita please!"

Wearing super cute boots, sandals and heels can be a no-no
Because your center of balance will change as your uterus begins to grow.

You might put your dirty glass in your purse and your keys in the sink
Forgetfulness is common in pregnancy so don't worry about what others think.

During pregnancy you have lush hair and a maternal glow
This is one of the most amazing times your body will ever know.

While you are pregnant please don't smoke or drink
They can do more damage to your little one than you think.

When the doctor starts to check to see if you are dilated
Your big belly makes it uncomfortable and you may feel violated.

Don't worry if your dilation progress each week is slow
Your baby is just comfortable and is taking extra time to grow.

Chapter Two

Labor

Don't worry much about your
water breaking at the mall
It could be a gush of water, or a
trickle of not much at all.

When your contractions start coming, wait
until they are five minutes apart
You will know it is time when you feel it
deep in your heart.

When you get to the hospital stay calm and
nice
Because your attitude can make your nurses
be like sugar or spice.

Epidural and pain meds depend on what you
want to do
But I would definitely take the easier way if I
were you.

Once labor starts your body leaks and does
things you didn't know it could
On second thought...it will do things that you
never hoped it would.

If the doctor breaks your water it will leak
onto the sheet
But the nurse will clean it up before you and
baby meet.

There is one thing that most women worry
about in labor too
And that is pushing so hard that you
accidentally go poo.

Don't worry about it if it happens and you
make a mess
After your baby is born you will really care
less.

The contractions will come quickly and may
cause pain
Just keep thinking about the love you are
about to gain.

If you think you are a modest woman, be
prepared not to be
During labor your "stuff" is on display for
everyone to see.

If your baby is large, your doctor may cut you
down "there"
The cut will be much better than a painful
tear.

Chapter Three

Birth and Beyond

You push and push and push until you see
your baby emerge
The memories of pain and gross fluids your
brain will eventually purge.

Your baby is then laid up close to you on your
chest
The bond you immediately feel is nothing
short of being the best.

When your baby's gaze meets yours and it
hears your voice
You know the gift of life is the ultimate gift
and choice.

You may freak out as your doctor does the
apgar test
Don't worry, they do it every day and they
know what is best.

You may or may not circumcise due to your
religious belief
Just having a healthy baby boy is a wonderful
relief.

If you decide to breastfeed you will be put to
a test
To teach your child to properly latch onto
your breast.

One thing after childbirth that no woman
wants or needs
Is that 10 days to 6 weeks of heavy vaginal
bleed.

After labor your baby is in diapers and you
will be too
To catch all of that wonderful after pregnancy
goo.

While you are in the hospital try to get lots of
rest
At home, functioning on lack of sleep is put
to the test.

Right after labor you are left with a saggy
belly
Laugh hard and it *will* jiggle like a bowl of
jelly.

The nurses will push on your tummy to make
sure everything is out
Your tummy is tired and sore so it makes you
want to shout!

Don't worry about your
husband thinking you no longer look great
You just gave birth to his child so he loves
that extra weight.

Afterwards it is sometimes difficult to go poo
So definitely take the medicine the doctor
gives to you.

You might have stretch marks on your belly,
thighs, and ass
But don't worry, with time the redness will
pass.

If your baby cries your breasts may leak milk
quick
Sometimes it is a little bit, whereas other
times it's thick.

Post Partum Depression maybe something
you go through
So make sure to have friends and family near
to support you.

When you get home everything for the two of
you will be new
But even if you screw up, your baby will still
love you.

Don't freak out if you think
you did something wrong
Motherhood is new and you
will learn as you go along.

You will be so exhausted and you really need
some sleep
But your mommy instinct will keep you up to
hear every baby peep.

So when your baby takes a nap you really
should too
I know it will be hard when there is so much
to do.

If you breastfeed your nipples will be at first
sore to the touch
But you really won't care because you love
your child so much.

Breastfeeding might make your nipples crack
and bleed
So nipple creams will be something you
definitely need.

When you start to wean from breastfeeding, it
may be hard to let go

Because as a mother it
is a bond only you and
your child know.

Brushing your teeth and taking showers are a
luxury from your past

If you get to do them now you
better do them fast!

Your baby's first poops are really black and
thick
Get ready mom, most of the time
the poop makes daddy sick.

You may even see your husband
gravel, plead and beg
To not clean up the poop creeping
down your baby's leg.

One thing that can be gross and expensive is a
baby diaper rash
Keep your baby clean or the creams will cost
you lots of cash.

When changing a little boy, quickly cover the
"wee-wee"
If you don't, you might end up with a face full
of "pee-pee".

Diapers start to look like the baby food they eat
Cleaning up a green pea diaper isn't necessarily a treat.

Never leave your baby alone on the changing table, couch or bed
It could cause a very serious injury to your little one's head.

Temperature is taken easier in the rear
So lube it up, smile and stick it in
without fear.

To prevent SIDS, laying your
baby on its back is best
Each night your maternal paranoia is put to
the test.

Some people are against using a blanket
swaddled tight
If you don't swaddle, get used to very little
sleep at night.

You can bathe your baby in the tub or even in
the sink
Either location will be more fun than you
could ever think!

When giving a bath beware of water in the
ears
And buy baby shampoo that doesn't cause
tears.

Baby nails grow at a quick pace
Keep them short so he
doesn't scratch his face.

Your baby may need to eat every two hours to
be happy and fine
Making, cleaning, and warming bottles
requires an assembly line.

Make sure you take a pacifier for your child
wherever you go
Keep them clean and sanitized so bacteria and
germs don't grow.

Being quiet while your baby sleeps is a big
mistake
Because then the tiniest noise they hear will
make them wake.

Your heart will break when they get shots and
cry
Especially when they look up at you like,
"mommy why?".

Don't leave your child unattended on the
couch or bed
Or he might roll off and
bump their little head.

Sometimes it takes a while to find the right pediatrician
They need to be knowledgeable and have lots of tricks like a magician.

Crying and pulling at the ear raises the question
Does my little angel have an ear infection?

Little colds and ear infections may happen a lot to your baby
The constant worry and doctor visits might make you a little crazy.

Carrying your baby in its car seat can tone
your arms faster
Be careful in stores, swinging it can cause a
messy disaster.

Sending out a birth announcement to brag can
be so much fun
There are so many excellent choices it will be
hard to choose just one!

You love your baby so much you want it
attached to your hip
Be careful of the wobbly, unstable head,
because it might bust your lip.

Activity mats will help your child learn to roll
front to back
And when it comes to road trips to grandma's
they are really easy to pack.

When your baby has bad gas it
will scream and yelp
Holding, burping and bouncing
on your knee might help.

If you have pets, let them love on your child
They will protect him from others, tame and/
or wild.

Chest carriers and slings are great for going
to the zoo or the mall
It's comforting to know you can move your
hands freely and your baby won't fall.

It is so amazing when your baby shows you
it's first smile
It will leave you feeling warm and fuzzy for
more than just a while.

They smile and giggle when you play hide
and seek
It's a game you now want to play all day and
all week.

.

Cherish each and every boogery and slobbery kiss
As they grow up it will be one thing you will surely miss.

If your child has a special blanket or lovie always buy two
Because if you lost one then what the heck would you do?

When it comes to education start out right
By reading to your child each and every night.

Put all your extra change in a
piggy bank for school
They think the jingling
change sound is really cool.

Take your child to see Santa and the Easter
Bunny
Those pictures are important and often times
funny.

Get ready to watch Barney and Scooby Doo
Baby Einstein, Lilo and Stitch and Dora too!

Instead of one bag for a weekend trip you will
now need about eight
For diapers, wipes, food, toys, crib and a
baby gate.

One day your child will
decide to take off and crawl
So make sure to block the
stairs and all the outlets in
the wall.

The choice of baby formula will be up to you
Most come in powder, liquid and travel packs
too.

As your child grows there will be lots of toys
and noise
Getting you ready for slumber parties of little
girls or boys.

Storing your child's outgrown clothes can
sometimes be sad
Just remember the memories that all those
clothes had.

Use the baby book to write down each and
every milestone
So you can look back and reminisce when
your child is full grown.

A digital camera is something that you will
always want to pack
Catch every "first" you can because you can't
get those back.

You will spend lots of money on photo paper
and on ink
Buying your own photo printer will be
cheaper than you think.

Start putting things in scrapbooks, they can be
lots of fun
You will have a sense of accomplishment
when they are done.

Chapter Four

Pregnancy Complaints

With pregnancy there are many issues and complaints
And sometimes discomfort and physical restraint.

You might have stretching, soreness and an occasional spot
Acne, bloating, heartburn and sweating because you are hot.

You can be tired, dizzy, swollen, and constantly have to pee
Have headaches, cravings, rashes and always be thirsty.

Constipation, discharge, and skin with a horrible itch
These crazy symptoms can make any woman a witch.

After all this, when the 40 weeks is through
Each and every moment will have been worth it for you.

Every woman's pregnancy is different in many ways
So sit back, relax and enjoy each and every day.

Chapter Five

Mommy Must Haves

The Must Have Mommy Checklist

Food
- Formula
- Bottles
- Bottle sterilizer
- Bottle warmer
- Extra bottle nipples
- Breast pump
- Bottle brush
- Burp cloth
- Bibs
- Bottle bag for traveling
- Breast milk storage bags for freezer
- Dishwasher basket for nipples

<u>The Must Have Mommy Checklist</u>

<u>Clothing</u>
- Onesies
- Pajamas with zippers
- Footie pajamas
- Pajama gowns
- Winter hats
- Summer hats
- Sunglasses
- Socks
- Mittens/gloves -to stop them from scratching their faces
- Jackets with hoods for cold weather
- Hangers
- Sleeping gowns

<u>The Must Have Mommy Checklist</u>

<u>Nursery</u>
- Crib
- Changing table
- Waterproof pads for crib
- Changing table cover
- Cotton balls
- Diapers
- Cotton swabs
- Wipes
- Nail clippers
- Powder
- Baby nail file
- Lotion
- Rash cream
- Vaseline
- Medicines
- Alcohol for umbilical stump
- First aid/Safety kit
- Swaddle blanket
- Extra sheets for srib
- Chair for rocking your baby to sleep
- Diaper pail
- Humidifier
- Baby books for bedtime
- Mobile for crib
- Baby monitor
- Breastfeeding Pillow

The Must Have Mommy Checklist

Bath Time
- Infant tub
- Shampoo
- Body wash
- Lotion
- Wash cloths
- Towels
- Robe/hoodies
- Bath toys
- Container to hold bath toys
- Water thermometer
- Flexible edge shampoo rinse cup
- Knee pad for your knees while bathing baby
- Faucet cover
- Pocket shower curtain liner (great for hiding things)

The Must Have Mommy Checklist

Diaper Bag

- Diapers
- Wipes
- Medicines
- Burp cloths
- Bibs
- Socks
- Hats
- Nail clippers
- Pacifiers
- Bottle
- Toys
- Travel packs of formula
- Snacks
- Tissues for runny noses
- Hand wipes/Sanitizer
- Extra shirt for mom
- Changing mat
- 2 changes of baby clothes

The Must Have Mommy Checklist

Gear

- Infant car seat
- Swing
- Bouncy seat
- High chair
- Booster seat
- Stroller
- Exersaucer
- Walker
- Pack N Play
- Bassinet
- Mirror for car
- Jumper
- Crib
- Changing table
- Rocking chair

The Must Have Mommy Checklist

Other Necessities

- Toys
- Blankets
- Sheets
- Books
- Movies
- Photo albums
- Onesies
- Sleeping gowns
- Footie pajamas with zippers
- Socks
- Hats
- Baby sunglasses
- Aspirators (one from the hospital is the best)
- Teething rings
- Thermometers
- Labels for all clothing, toys, bottles and pacifiers
- Pacifier clips
- Digital camera and Video camera

The Must Have Mommy Checklist

Safety Items

- Outlet plugs
- Cabinet locks
- Baby gates
- Door knob locks
- Corner pads
- Drawer locks
- Stove shields
- Bumper for fireplace
- Sharp corner covers

Medicines/Creams

- Infant Tylenol
- Teething Gel
- Neosporin for Circumcision
- Tummy Tablets
- Baby sunscreen
- Infant Motrin
- Saline for nose
- Nipple cream
- Diaper cream

Chapter Six
Mommies
Favorite
Memories

The "Firsts" for Mommy

- The first pregnancy symptom_____

- The first bout of morning sickness_____

- The first we told the news _____

- The first craving_____

- The first body change_____

- The first Doctor appointment_____

- The First Ultrasound_____

The "Firsts" for Mommy

- The First Time You Saw Your Childs Profile_____

- The First Kick_____

- The First Maternity Item You Purchased_____

- The First Piece of Nursery Furniture You Purchased_____

- The First Nesting Syndrome_____

- The First Gift Purchased For Your Baby_____

- The First Contraction_____

Dates for Mommy to Remember

- Date of the Positive Pregnancy Test_____

- Date the Doctor Confirmed Your Pregnancy_____

- Date You Were Expected to Give Birth_____

- Date you Registered for Your Baby Shower_____

- Where You Registered_____

- Date of Your Baby Shower_____

- Location of the Baby Shower

- Person(s) Who Hosted the Baby Shower _____

- Date Your Child Was Born_____

Chapter Seven

Mommies Measurements

Mommies Measurements

<u>Weight</u>

Pre-Pregnancy_____

Day of Childbirth_____

One Month After Birth_____

	<u>Pre-Preg</u>	**<u>Childbirth</u>**	**<u>Month Birth</u>**
Thighs			
Hips			
Bottom			
Breasts			
Shoe Size			

52963575R00032

Made in the USA
Lexington, KY
17 June 2016